"Elder Berries"

Verses for and about Senior Citizens

by
Beatrice Haniford

Illustrations by
Ronald F. W. Robinson

Published by **Creative Writing by**

"ELDER" BERRIES

Copyright © 1996 by
Beatrice Haniford

ISBN 0-9655347-0-7

All rights reserved. No part of this book may be reproduced or transmitted in any form or by any means, electronic or mechanical, including photocopying, recording, or by any information storage and retrieval system, without permission in writing from the publisher.

Printed in United States of America by
MECCA PRINTING, TONAWANDA, NY

Dedicated to my wonderful family - my children and grandchildren - who must contend with me as an "Elder" Berry

CONTENTS

A Senior's Lament	1
Wither Do I Wander?	2
Winter	3
Keys	4
The Wedding	6
Tears	7
Warming Up	8
Table Talk	9
What Did You Say?	11
Conversation	12
The Trip	14
Retirement	18
Tales Of The Beach Walker	20
To Love Again	21
Cards, Anyone?	23
A Change in Plans	25
Remember?	26
Part Smart	27
Mirror, Mirror On The Wall	28
A Dose Of Nonsense	29
A Pressing Matter	30
Teacher, Teacher	31
Ah, Sweet Mystery Of Life	32
The Last Ride	33
Longevity	34

The Movies	35
Hormones	37
Aging	38
TV And Me	39
Warm Memories	40
Music?	41
Aspirations	43
The Spare Room	45
Bye-Bye Buy Buy	47
Comprenez-Vous?	49
Love At The Laundromat	50
Values	52
Best Friends	54
Dress Code	56
The Test	58
Proud Mom	61
The Big Game	62
Doctor, Doctor	64
Progress	66
I'll Bite	68
The Lottery	69
The Senior Prom	71
Soliloquy	73
Car Trouble	74
The Grandsons	76
Class Distinction	79
Finale	80

A Senior's Lament

I'd been forgetting
So much these days
And I was determined
To change my ways
So I drove to the Mall
Parked and knew
This time I'd remember
What I should do
I turned off the wipers
The heater - the lights
Locked the doors
Achieved new heights
"I CAN coach my brain, "
I said aloud
Yes indeed
I was very proud
I knew exactly
Where I had parked
The space - the place
I'd clearly marked
Then I shopped
Just like a star
And returned to find -
My keys in the car!

Whither Do I Wander?

I walked into the kitchen
I know not why
I stood before the fridge
And heaved a sigh
What did I want?
Why was I here?
Will I remember
If I persevere?
Guess there's nothing to do
But walk back to the den
Perk up my memory
And try again

Winter

I am concerned
My age is showing
I don't want to go out
When it's cold and blowing
If I am tempted
I quell the desire
Grab a book
And sit by the fire
I dislike the snow
Think sleet is appalling
I'm dreadfully afraid
Of slipping and falling
"Winter Wonderland" is not for me
I don't care to shovel
And I can't ski
But I've conceived a thought
For what comfort it will bring
When I awake each morning
It's a day nearer Spring

Keys

Do keys have legs?
They're never where I put them
Some House Gremlin
Seems to uproot them
I'm sure I place them in one spot
But when I need them
They are "not"
I look in pockets
I look in drawers
Maybe they dropped
I'm on all fours -
I can't start the car
Without my keys
I'll look in the pantry
Get off my knees
The hunt goes on
And what is worse
I'm sure they were resting
In my purse
Those naughty keys
Running around
I've nowhere to go
Until they are found

So back to my handbag
My woes not forgotten
And there they are
Down at the bottom
The first time I looked
They just weren't there
Keys MUST have legs
They go everywhere!

The Wedding

My daughter wanted a big wedding
"You shall have it, " we both said
We'll call the caterer tomorrow
To plan a glorious spread
Everything was beautiful
The flowers, the food, her dress
No expense was spared at all
It was a huge success
We borrowed to make it possible
But did it with love and good will
Didn't even regret it
When we saw the exorbitant bill
Now a year has passed
And life has taken a strange course
We are still paying
My daughter is getting a divorce

Tears

"You're too old to drive,"
My children said
So I gave my car
To my grandson, Ted
Soon after
My husband died
I just stayed home
And cried and cried
The family tried to comfort me
But didn't get too far
Because I wasn't crying for my husband
I was grieving for my car

Warming Up

My husband and I
Quarrel day and night
I know I'm never wrong
He thinks he's always right
It's not about money, family or sex
We just bicker and badger
Until we are wrecks
It's not about politics
Or anything like that
Our constant conflict is
The thermostat
I push it up
He puts it down
He removes his coat
I don an extra gown
I am cold
He is hot
And when I'm hot
He is not
It's like a race
But no one will beat
The finish I guess
Will be a "dead heat"

Table Talk

My family's coming to dinner
It will be such fun to cook
I'll use my best silver and china
How lovely the table will look
I'm buying wine for the occasion
We're sure to have a toast
And I'm studying my old recipe
For a delicious, succulent roast
It will be a pleasure
To whip up such a treat
Then suddenly I remember
Gwendolyn won't eat meat
She's a vegetarian
I'll have to make something with cheese
But Tom's watching his cholesterol
I don't know whom to please
Perhaps I'll roast a turkey
But no - I can't do that
Patty doesn't like white meat
And says the dark meat is too fat
Of course I'll make my chicken soup
But it's not good without salt
And Henry's pressure is so high
He's careful to a fault

Salmon might be nice
It's a savory dish
But if I remember correctly
Theodore doesn't eat fish
I'll make a colorful salad
Remember though not to use dill
Florence says she's allergic
It always makes her ill
Jeremy doesn't like onions
Simply won't touch tomatoes
Andrea says she's putting on weight
And is staying off potatoes
Maybe I'll make some pasta
But that too will make her stout
After careful consideration
I think I'll take them out

What Did You Say?

My husband claimed I didn't hear well
And should get a hearing aid
But I know - he spoke too low
On purpose - I'm afraid
When he had to repeat
He fumed and grumbled
Between you and me
He always mumbled
But I gave in
Wear an auricular crutch
And now my mate says
I hear TOO much

Conversation

I have six friends
All of them dears
And we have been friends
For year and years
We go way back
To talk of dates
Love - sex
And choosing mates
Having babies
Obstetricians
Diapers - colic
Pediatricians
Talking - walking
Falling - bumps
Chicken Pox - Measles
Colds - Mumps
Birthday parties
Learning tools
Toys - books
Nursery Schools
Meetings
Possessions
Mortgages
Recessions

Troubled
Teens
Problems
Of the In-Betweens
Love
Of knowledge
Where to send the kids
To College
<u>Their</u> sex
<u>Their</u> dates
<u>Their</u> loves
<u>Their</u> mates
Menopause
The Russians
Parents - Worries
Heated discussions
And now - pains and aches
Frustration
Cataracts and
Constipation
We call ourselves
The Lucky Seven
Wonder what we'll talk about
When we all go up to Heaven

The Trip

My daughter lives a distance away
I left to visit her
Last Saturday
I traveled by air
It was much too far
To make the trip
By motor car
I arrived at the airport
(I was driven by my son)
My "carry-on" was heavy
Must have weighed a ton
It was full of goodies
An applesauce cake
And lots of other lovelies
The kind mothers take
I sat in the terminal
The plane was late
There was nothing to do
But calmly wait
Still I was nervous
I felt no surety
And strangely enough
Didn't pass security

There was contraband somewhere
I found it in my pocket
I had forgotten to remove
My antique metal locket
But soon we took off
Everything was intact
Until the pilot announced
"We're turning back
There's trouble with the engine
Nothing serious I say
We'll soon have it fixed -
Sorry for the delay."
And so I sat 'til it was dark
When given the signal
To re-embark
By then, of course
I'd missed my connection
So the airline "computerized"
Another selection -
At last I was there
So glad to see
The entire clan
Welcoming me
I unpacked my bag
The cookies were squashed
The applesauce cake
Quite applesauced

But the next day we laughed
Talked, exchanged views
Feasted and caught up
With the family news
When Monday came
They hurried off to work
Didn't even wait
For the coffee to perk
I had nothing to do
But sit and sew
While at home I was always
On the go
I couldn't go out
It was constantly pouring
The days were long
It was really boring
Then after a week
It was time to return
The flight back home
My troubled concern
There was turbulence
Lots of waiting
I found it all
So enervating

I came to the conclusion
I was too old
To jaunt and journey
Besides, I'd caught cold
I was tired
My nerves were unraveling
This I decided
Was the end of my traveling
But when my daughter called
To say. "Come soon again,"
I started planning
And answered, "When?"

Retirement

When I was young
I aspired
To be financially firm
When I retired
I invested my money
I scrimped and saved
Lived most carefully
Temptation I waived
When the day arrived
I was truly elated
But suddenly I found
Costs were inflated
Interest was lowered
Expenses increased
My security was threatened
My enthusiasm ceased
Then I had a heart attack
And my wife got thin
Constantly wondering
Where she had been
It wasn't at all
As I had planned
In fact it was more
Than I could stand

I realized somehow
That good times were for the young
That earlier years
Were designed for fun
Old age just isn't
A bed of clover
And if I had
To do it over
Would it be different?
Less work and more play?
I think not
I'd live the same way

Tales Of The Beach Walker

I walk along the Beach alone
See couples sauntering
      hand-in-hand
Having lost my mate
I am filled with envy
And wonder if they know
How fortunate they are -
"Cherish each other, " I say
      as they pass
They look at me
      strangely!

To Love Again

Is it possible
To love again?
To know the thrill
You once knew then?
The quickening heartbeat
As his footsteps near
The kiss - the warmth
Of "How are you, dear? "
The strength of his arms
His touch on your breast
The years disappear
As to him you are pressed
Soft talk
Of mem'ries sweet
Confessions - confidences
Tales of defeat
Happiness - fulfillment
The beauty of belonging
Replacing the void
The loneliness - the longing

No plans for tomorrow
Just "May today last! "
A new life for both
A feeling to grasp
Knowing it IS possible
To love again
To relive the wonder
You once knew then

Cards, Anyone?

For years I've gone to my bridge club
It meets every week
And lately I have enjoyed
A delightful winning streak
But it matters not
If I win or lose
It's the place I go
For the latest news
We talk -
We play
There's always gobs
We have to say
We seldom remember
What's been bid
And once in a while
May even renege
Adding honor count
Can be a chore
And we usually forget
To look at the score

"Whose deal?"
Is a familiar line
And "Result" is the system
We use all the time
But we do have fun
Without Bridge decorum
And we end each session
With apologies to Goren!

A Change In Plans

I've arthritis in my back
Gout in my toe
I really can't get up
I'm hurting so
My sinus is clogged
My toenail is ingrown
And I'm feeling rather dizzy -
(Oh there goes the phone)
"Hello, Amy dear
Will I dine?
And will I play Canasta?
Of course! What time? "

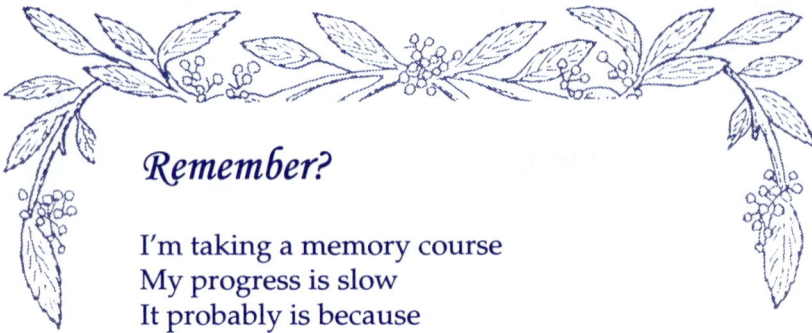

Remember?

I'm taking a memory course
My progress is slow
It probably is because
I forget to go!

Part Smart

I've had a heart transplant
Two artificial knees
A hip replacement
So I can walk with ease
My kidney is my brother's
Had a corneal transplant to see
And what I want to know is -
"Am I me?"

Mirror, Mirror On The Wall

I look in the mirror
Don't like what I see
"A little old lady"
Heavens - it's me!

A Dose Of Nonsense

I am supposed to take my medicine
But I can't unscrew the lid
I've been fussing with it an hour
I really "overdid"
It's child-proof I know
And I feel just like a fool
But my grandson will open it
When he comes from Nursery School

A Pressing Matter

I am a whiz with the iron
Every pleat in place
But I can't get the wrinkles
Out of my face!

Teacher, Teacher

I taught school for thirty years
Then I happily retired
I thought fun and freedom
Were all that I required
But I don't enjoy retirement
What I find instead
Is that I can't get teaching school
Out of my head
If I wake up late
Though feeling hale and hearty
In my mind
I mark myself "tardy"
When I'm viewing TV
And don't pay attention
I immediately think
I should be sent to "Detention"
I call housework "homework"
Keep striving for goals
Named my home baked biscuits
"Honor Rolls"
I'd better change my thinking
If I don't, I'm afraid
I'll have to give myself
A failing grade

Ah, Sweet Mystery of Life

My grandmother
Is a menace on the road
She ignores most stop signs
Has no safety code
She cannot see well
Neither does she hear
Yet she has a license
To start the car and steer
It's amazing
She's still alive
But she's never had an accident
And I've had five

The Last Ride

Funerals are so costly
The price of monuments high
I better live a long life
I can't afford to die

Longevity

I lived very carefully
Thought I'd have enough
When I was old
And the going was rough
But now I'm in my eighties
And life's not so sunny
Living this long
I have more years than money

The Movies

The movies these days
Are as violent as can be
Full of sex
And impropriety
I remember so well
The earlier days
When nothing got past
The Censor - Will Hayes
Unwed mothers usually died
And the sin they committed
Was only implied
Occasionally we saw
Couples in bed
If they of course
Were properly wed
The scene was X-rated
And what is more
One leg of the male
Had to appear on the floor
Villains got their just do
And naturally swearing
Was strictly taboo

The art was clean
There was nothing lewd
And no one was ever
Seen in the nude
If an actress wore a negligee
It would excite
And keep us all imagining
What happened that night
But now is now
And that was then
And I'm off
To see a movie again
I'm going with my daughter
So I'll probably fake it
Make believe I'm hip
And really can take it
But I'll be shocked
From here to Mars
And the Reviewer tomorrow
Will give it "5 stars"

Hormones

A fiery flash
Brushes my skin
A bodily inferno
Comes from within
Encompassing
My entire being
My flesh feels flaccid
As if fleeing
From me
I want to tear off my clothes
Cool my brow
I'm in the throes
Of a flaming Hell that soon passes
Leaving only the cause
An ending - a beginning
Menopause!

Aging

I cannot believe
I am the wife
Of this man
Who once was my life
He was so bright
So strong
Now he is just a shell
Drifting along
Sands of confusion
Dependent
Oblivious to the past
So resplendent
With love and living
Family
And giving
Here, a flaw in God's great design
"Alzheimer's"
The tragedy of time!

TV And Me

I'm always watching television
The good stuff and the creepy
And often while I'm viewing it
I seem to get so sleepy
I'm into a movie
A "sit-com" - a play
And right in the middle
I snooze away
The tube blasts on
And when I awake
There's a talk show or chef
Baking a cake
It's most disturbing
I profess
I never know
How the plots progress
Why doesn't some sponsor
For the money it spends
Present an hour
Of just "Program ENDS"

Warm Memories

I've lost my virility
And feel very sad
The doctor said, "Don't worry
Think of the joys you've had
It will be a comfort
To recall passions of the past
The best things in life you know
Seldom ever last."
So I did
What the doctor said
Remembered the pleasures
Of my marital bed
The torrid nights
The matinees
The excitement and lust
Of earlier days
I followed instructions
Right to the letter
The memories ARE good
But sex is better

Music?

I really abhor "Rock'n Roll"
The noise - the beat - the bong
Don't know how the young folks bear it
They play it all day long
And when they dance
They look so wild
Overwrought
And over-riled
It's not refined
It's not polished
I really wish
It could be abolished
Then I remember
What my parents thought
Of the songs we loved
The tempo we sought
The "Big Band Sound"
Was part of my day
Artie Shaw - Sammy Kaye
Wonderful tunes
That had pizzazz
The great Count Basie
And all that jazz

We'd have the radio
Blaring away
Jitterbug in the hall
To my mother's dismay
And I can still hear
My father saying
"That's not music
You are playing
It's brassy - it's brazen
It's full of faults
Why can't you kids
Just play a waltz?"
Seems if each generation
Swings to the times
And expresses in music
Worldly signs
Maybe thirty years hence
Our young ones
Will live a life less tense
There won't be the pain
The pressures they've met
And they'll go back to dancing
The Minuet

Aspirations

When I was young
I dreamed of fortune and fame
Mine would be
A respected name
I'd write great novels
A prize-winning play
With "Standing Room Only"
When it reached Broadway
But I fell in love - married
Settled down
Had children
And moved to a very small town
Excuses galore
Clouded my writing
Life was beautiful
But not that exciting
"I'd create, " I thought
"When the children were older
Or when summer passed
And the weather was colder"
There were problems on hand
That needed attacking
But in my heart I knew
Something was lacking

Perhaps it was talent
Or perhaps I was afraid
That I really and truly
Couldn't make the grade -
I never wrote the novels
I never wrote the plays
I never had riches
I was a stranger to praise
But suddenly I realized
When my children gathered one day
That here was where
My aspired fame lay
These were my jewels
The fortune I possess
I looked at them and knew
I had been a success

The Spare Room

We had a problem
Didn't know what to do
My daughter wrote from College
She'd be home with boyfriend, Stu
"We'll arrive about eight
Depending on the weather
And don't make up the spare room
Stu and I bunk together."
Well, I was startled
But stayed calm and aloof
While my hubby roared violently
"Not under my roof!"
Maybe, I thought,
We shouldn't judge
But my husband was adamant
He wouldn't budge
So I called my daughter
Tried to explain
She said, "Dad's so old-fashioned
He gives me a pain

So make up the spare room
That will be fine. "
And they appeared
Full of laughter
About a quarter of nine
It was great to see them
We talked until late
They kissed goodnight
As if on a date
Liz went to her room
Stu to his
Next morning Stu was still in the spare room
And so was Liz

Bye-Bye Buy Buy

I awoke with a smile
For a special reason
I was going shopping
For the holiday season
Gifts for my children
And grandchildren too
A winter treat
I looked forward to
So off I went
To my favorite store
With expectations of buying
Presents galore
I found a salesgirl
(This was perfection)
I knew she'd help me
With my selection
"Something a five year old would wear."
She looked at me blankly
And replied, "Over there."
I rummaged through the rack
Found a frock that was nice
I thought I would take it
'Til I saw the price
There were other dresses

That were better buys
But I didn't like the colors
And I wasn't sure of size
So I wandered a little further
Found sweaters for the boys
Then I remembered
They wanted toys
The electronic kind
I'd seen a few
But which ones they wanted
I hadn't a clue
For Bill and Bess
Something for their home
Bess loves silver
Bill prefers chrome
It presents a problem
Oh what the heck!
I think I'll go home
Send each one a check

Comprenez-Vous?

I majored in languages
Latin and French
My study of Spanish
Was very intense
In German and Italian
I did my best
And I studied Greek
With classic zest
But a new language
Has come to be
One that completely
Flabbergasts me
"Ram - Rom - Pixel - Snobal
Asch - Modem - Nexus - Cobal"
It's computer vocabulary
Very much in demand
But I'm too old
To understand
"Radix - Fortran - Pascal - Glitch"
It's all too much
For my elderly wits
I will need a Roto - Rooter
To dig the lingo
Of a computer

Love At The Laundromat

He went to the Laundromat
For the very first time
The passing of his wife
Made him define
What had to be done
Now that he was alone -
He was keeping house
And didn't own
A washer and dryer
Didn't know how they worked
Thought he'd inquire -
Then a very sweet lady
Said, "I'll help you now
It's an easy procedure
I'll show you how. "
He put in the coins
Did what he was told
And suddenly
Didn't feel so alone and old
He sat down and talked
About his dear wife who had died
She told of her late husband
While their loads of clothes dried

Week after week
They made the scene
Exchanged life stories
As they used each machine
And now every Monday
Whatever the weather
They bring one basket
Of laundry - together

Values

I have many possessions
Countless valuable things
China - sterling - linens
Several diamond rings
And always had pleasure in knowing
There would come a day
When my children would inherit
This priceless array
So I summoned the family together
Looked proudly at my heirs
What joy there'd be in announcing
That everything was theirs
My daughter looked so pretty
My son handsome and gallant
But both replied in unison,
"There's nothing that we want.
We use paper napkins
Plastic dishes are just fine
And if we want to entertain
We go out to dine

Your rings are ostentatious
We'd be up for ridicule
If we appeared anywhere
With a diamond jewel
So you just keep enjoying them
Until your fatal date
And we'll be around to manage
The sale of your estate."

Best Friends

I have an old friend
Who's so good to me
She's always around
Talks incessantly
I find her presence
Comfortably nice
And she seems to give me
Sound advice
Often when
I am in doubt
Think I shouldn't do
What I am about
She'll give me courage
Say, "You won't rue it
Don't just lie there
Get up and do it. "
Or sometimes
When I'm feeling sad
She'll say, "Shame on you
Think of the blessings
You have had. "

We never argue
She never talks back
She compensates
For whatever I lack
We converse day and night
In fact - she's never
Out of my sight
It's the one person
Upon whom I rely
Know who it is?
It is I!

Dress Code

When we were growing up
(With a bit of persuasion)
We dressed up
For every special occasion
My mother would say,
"We're having a guest
Go upstairs and put on
Your 'Sunday Best' "
The boys would wear suit coats
Ties and shirts
The girls wore dresses
Or pleated skirts
Today parents may utter
The very same words
But "Sunday Best"
Is just for nerds
The children wear T-Shirts
Oversized
And the dirtier their jeans
The more they are prized

Expensive sneakers
Are their pride
And the boys wear
Baseball caps - even inside
They look disheveled
Unkempt - never dressy
Wonder if that's why
The world is so messy!

The Test

I had a lovely marriage
With five children to raise
Three girls - two boys
All worthy of my praise
I had to work real hard
To keep my family going
Did a bit of moonlighting
While all the kids were growing
I sent them through college
And until on their own
Helped each one get started
With a fatherly loan
Well now the years have passed
There's no one home
My wife is gone too
And I'm all alone
So I decided recently
It would be so very nice
If I lived with one of the children
For the rest of my life
I called my first-born daughter
(Grace and I were very close)
Told her what I had in mind
That I was lonely and morose

Grace said, "I'm sorry, Dad,
But Fred's not very well
We think our home's too big
And that this is the time to sell
We've rented an apartment
With not a room to spare."
"Oh, that's all right," I said to Grace
"I'll call your sister Claire."
Claire was gracious
As anyone could be
But said, "Oh Daddy, you cannot live with me
I've taken a new position
I'll be a traveling V.P.
It really did pay off, Dad
To get my PhD"
That night I went to dinner
At my daughter Betsy's house
She was the youngest of the brood
And gentle as a mouse
She listened most attentively
Then said, "Some day, maybe,
But right now I don't have any room
We're expecting a new baby."
"How about the boys?" I thought
We always got along
I'll talk to Roger very soon
He's sensible and strong

I was truly disappointed
When Roger said to me
"Oh Dad, I'd like that very much
But I'm afraid it cannot be
Our Jane is getting a divorce
Her life is full of sorrow
So she's bringing her two little ones
And moving in tomorrow."
That left only Peter
He's my bachelor son
Who has a huge apartment
Big enough for more than one
But when I met with Peter
He said he'd give it a whirl
However at this very time
He was living with a girl
So I guess I'll stay all alone
Keep in touch with the children
By telephone
And next time I live
In my grand husband role
I think I'll practice -
Birth Control

Proud Mom

Next week, at a luncheon
They're honoring my son
A prize in Physics
For the work he has done
I think it's because
He's proved some rules
About follicles
Or molecules -
Whatever - it must be
Something scientific
That son of mine
Is truly terrific
Oh yes, I've been invited
And of course I'll attend
Sit there proudly
And sort of pretend
I understand
Although I haven't a clue
I'll smile and look wise
As if I knew
And I'll brag to my friends
Tell them how it was
And pray they don't ask me
What my son does

The Big Game

My wife and I
Are very compatible
But when it comes to TV
Our home's
Inhabitable
I watch sports
Every phase
While my wife likes only
Music and plays
We each have
Our own TV
Do our viewing
Separately
But recently
During stormy weather
My dear wife suggested
We stay together
"I'll be the martyr
Strange as it may seem
I'll sit with you
And cheer for your team."

So we curled up on the couch
Hand-in-hand
And I queried with concern,
"Will you understand?"
She said, "Of course
Football's fun."
Yelled, "Come on, Bills,
Make a Home Run!"

Doctor, Doctor

My friend and physician
Passed away
I was without a doctor
To my dismay
And one day
I became unwell
Ran a fever
Had a fainting spell
Whom would I see?
I was filled with tension
I needed antibiotics
And immediate attention
So I phoned Dr. A
Recommended by relations
But Dr. A wasn't taking
Any new patients
I then called Dr. B
(I was feeling worse)
But I got no further
Than the office nurse
Dr. C was available
But not today
She was taking appointments
For the middle of May
Dr. D would see me

At last! That was great!
Though I was told "payment in advance"
And that I might have to wait
And wait I did
Feeling the same
When suddenly I was beckoned
By my first name
I was examined
Then told to see
Another doctor for an EKG
Still another for an MRI
Plus an EEG
I didn't know why
So many tests
When I simply knew
I was suffering
From a bad case of flu
But I went the alphabetical route
To protect the doctor
From a malpractice suit
Well - two weeks have passed
And thanks to nature and time
And some medication
I'm feeling fine
Modern medicine's wonderful
That is a fact
But I'd be happier
If my old doctor were back

Progress

With a patch on my eye
I cannot forget
I am a member
Of the Cataract Set
I've had no-stitch surgery
A lens implant
Phacoemulsification
(The discomfort was scant)
And I think of the time
Many years back
When my dad had the removal
Of *his* cataract
Hospitalized for two weeks
He just lay in bed
For fear he might move
There were sandbags at his head
Today - it's so simple
I can bend, bow or jar
And in just a few days
I'll be driving my car

At this rate of progress
It would not be a surprise
If some day, in the case
Of ailing eyes
Folks would just SIGN in
Have their cataracts removed
At a CATARACT DRIVE-IN

I'll Bite

I've had
Many misadventures
Since I've been
Wearing dentures
The dentist says
They fit fine
But I know they don't
Because they're mine
Crunchy candy
I cannot chew
And corn-on-the-cob
Is strictly taboo
My conclusion ?
Really ruthless
I'd rather suffer
Than be toothless!

The Lottery

I never had much money
But I dream about the day
When I will win the lottery
And the fortune it will pay
I plan to give to my family
A very healthy share
And of course I'll give to charity
Because I truly care
There'll be money for a new car
Nothing ostentatious
For living as a capitalist
I expect to be most gracious
I'll pay off the mortgage
Maybe move away
Take countless trips around the world
In the new role I will play
I'll use the money wisely
My concerns will never cease
I might even give a huge chunk
To guarantee world peace

But wait - here are the numbers
I have a chance to win
I may HAVE the lucky digits
Though the odds are very thin
I must listen closely
And do I have them? "Nope! "
But I'll buy another ticket
For where there's lottery - there's hope!

The Senior Prom

At the Senior Center
There was a dance
But there were no men -
Then I caught a glance
Of a male
At the door
I quickly glided
Across the floor -
Deciding to be bold
I approached this man
(Devious - that was me
With my little plan)
"Hello, " I said
Trying to look trimmer
"If you dance with me sir
I'll invite you to dinner. "
He must have been hungry
Because he said, "O.K. "
And though he was clumsy
We pranced away
We talked as we danced
He was full of pep
And I asked some questions
With his every misstep

"Have you been here before
Or are you a newcomer? "
He said, "I'm not a Senior
I'm Max Muffet, the plumber.
There's a leak in the kitchen
I was sent to fix
But business and pleasure
Sometimes can mix
So thanks for the dance
You're light on your feet
I'll be over for dinner
What time do we eat? "
So now I'll go home
Prepare a meal
Because dancing with ladies
Didn't appeal!

Soliloquy

We used to call her
"Crazy Kate"
She'd talk to herself
From early to late
Now that I'm old
And alone - I find
It's good to speak out
What's on your mind
I have ideas
That really glisten
So I say them aloud
Though there's no one to listen
Yes - I talk to myself
Before my thoughts get hazy
Maybe Kate
Wasn't so crazy!

Car Trouble

Can't buy a new car
I'm afraid
They cost much more
Than I paid
Years ago
For a beautiful home
And I'm too old
For an Auto Loan
So I'll fix up
My family transport
Make it as workable
As a Foreign import
I'll paint it
Put in new shocks
Get four tires
Repair the locks
Buy a battery
New brakes too
Tune up the motor
And when I'm through

My refurbished creation
Will cost as much
As my last operation
Wouldn't it be great
If some government star
Would inaugurate a plan
Called "Medicar?"

The Grandsons

I thought, "What a happy day
This will be
My grandsons are coming
To visit me"
I will baby sit
While my daughter shops
I'll feed them spinach
And huge Lamb Chops
We'll do puzzles - play games
Have a grand time
Taking care of young ones
Is where I shine
Well - they came
Looked so cute
Each one wearing
A new snow suit
They said, "Good-bye Mommie"
I knew we'd have fun
But these two little boys
Just wanted to run
Upstairs and downstairs
It was quite a race
With little old me
Keeping apace

Charging into the rec room
They created a gun
By placing a finger
On top of a thumb
"Bang Bang, " they cried
As they wildly fled
"Get down Grandma
Don't you know you're dead? "
My heart was aflutter
But I thought I'd be brave
Ask permission to arise
From my premature grave
"Come on, boys
I've a hunch
You both are ready
For my special lunch. "
So into the kitchen
They bolted with glee
But they didn't eat anything
Prepared by me
They wanted a Pizza
That was their diet
So we all went out
In order to buy it

It meant getting dressed
Helping with their boots
Wedging them into
Their handsome snow suits
But off we went
For the food they desired
And when we came home
I was truly tired
In moments the bell rang
My daughter returned
"Were they good Mom? " she asked
She was deeply concerned
"They were just dolls. "
I tactfully said
Then they went home
And I went to bed!

Class Distinction

I am a Senior Citizen
With benefits galore
I pay less at the theater
Get discounts at the store
I belong to the AARP
Collect Social
Security
Yes - I'm a Senior Citizen
But oh my gosh
You can keep all the benefits
I'd rather be a frosh

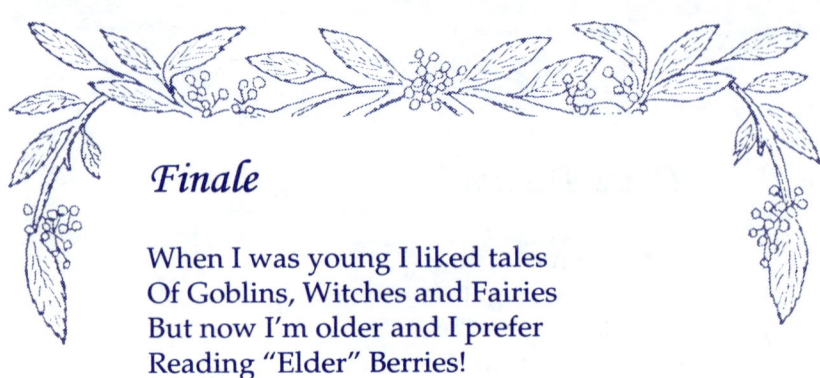

Finale

When I was young I liked tales
Of Goblins, Witches and Fairies
But now I'm older and I prefer
Reading "Elder" Berries!

ABOUT THE AUTHOR

Bea Haniford has been writing verses, plays and programs in Buffalo, NY, ever since she was 13 years old. Professionally, she has worked more than 25 years as a radio and television copywriter. After her retirement, she did free lance writing, mostly in advertising and public relations. Adventures of her many aging contemporaries motivated her to put their happenings into rhyme. Thus, "Elder" Berries!